AF322597

YOU 2.0

The Definitive Owner's Manual
To Changing Your Life

Mark A. Rosche

The Mark Rosche Group, LLC.

<u>TMRG</u>

Wake Forest, North Carolina

For information about The Mark Rosche Group, LLC.

PO Box 1593, Wake Forest, North Carolina 27587

Printed in the United States of America

First Edition, 2024

Library of Congress Control Number - Pending

Table of Contents

PROLOGUE

WoW!!! The past ten-or-so years have been quite a ride on the crazy train. Of all the things that have happened in our lives, our country and around the world, it would appear that the bad, stupid, ugly, crazy and evil have managed to take center stage throughout our world and become annoyingly mainstream.

Unfortunately, this has left too many people standing around with a form of PTSD. People feel lost, confused and depressed. Not knowing what to do or where to go.

Problem? Yes!

Relegated to a life of anxiety-ridden depression and underwhelming results? Of course not!

And that brings us to the topic of this book. If you're not happy with where your life is today, or if you're ok with your life today, but know there is something more for you, then this book was written just for you.

By the application of this book, your life will change. Things will get better. You will feel a sense of accomplishment and fulfillment as you transition to a "new you."

With that little bit of administrivia behind us, that new you is just around the corner. So let's get out of the starting gate and get this show on the road!

Mark

CHAPTER 1
YOU 1.0

Why You Are Where You Are And Who You Are

While this may sound a bit harsh, or maybe some philosophical mumbo jumbo, we all need to come to terms with why our lives are as they are today. The answer is simply, "Because of you. Your thinking, your beliefs, and your actions." You 1.0 is all about you!"

This is an Owner's Manual to your life's journey and how to make necessary changes. And I need to get you to a position where you understand what specifically got you to where you are today. Let's do a bit of personal introspection and see if we can determine what's going on here. Afterall, we need to understand where we are and how we got here today, to understand where we want to be tomorrow, and how to get there!

THE INTROSPECTION ASSIGNMENT

You are going to need a few hours or more of focused, quiet time. So let everyone know that you are on a personal journey to "You 2.0," and you need private time and space. Our first activity is to get into a state of "Flow."

For those of you that haven't heard of the Flow State, it was termed by psychologist Mihály Csikszentmihalyi in 1975. There are a lot of letters in that name to simply say, "flow" is a mental state when a person is performing some activity and is fully immersed in a feeling of energized focus. A state of fully assimilated, undistracted involvement and enjoyment of the process of the activity.

Have you ever been in a state where time did not exist? Hunger did not exist. Before you know it, 10-plus hours of activity/time had passed, and you weren't even aware of it? That is the flow state. You need to be in flow.

Many, many, many years ago, I was fully immersed and assimilated into the life of a performing musician and recording studio engineer. On numerous occasions, once we entered into the process of creating, performing, recording and mastering musical records, it was quite common that 16, 20, and at times more hours passed by. And we weren't even aware of what time it was. As long as "the necessities" were provided, we were good. It was a very intense, demanding, and creatively rewarding period of being in flow.

Now that you are negotiating yourself into a state of flow, go back to your earliest memories of life. Your goal is to document all good decisions and actions in your life and why/how they happened, and all the bad decisions and actions in your life, and why/how they happened. As you remember these experiences of your life, write down the who, what, when, where, how and whys of those decisions and actions you made. Fully integrate yourself into all those memories. See what you saw, said, smelled, heard, touched and felt. Emotionally ground yourself in every moment of those memories. Those memories must be palpable!

We need to understand all the intimate details of where, how and why we were successful and unsuccessful. Our goal in getting to You 2.0 is to massively replicate our success mentality and use it as a force multiplier by expanding those experiences into your conscious mind, today. Introspection is key. Really be there.

A simple T-Chart is all you need to get going.

Good Decisions and Actions	Bad Decisions and Actions
1	1
2	2
3	3
4	4
5	5
6	6

Figure 1

As the chart indicates, everything good goes on the left side of the chart, everything not-so-good on the right side.

This is an introspective assignment and is not meant to cast any value judgement on your life, decisions or actions. It is a simple definition of what you did to get where you are today. Once we know that, then we can easily create the journey to You 2.0.

By the time you get done with this assignment, you should have a few pages of an understanding of your "You 1.0 Journey" of getting to today.

Now go to your favorite stationary store and get a big 3-inch, 3-ring binder. Punch holes and put all documentation into the binder. You'll have all the necessary documentation to be able to write an autobiography when you are done.

With that assignment done, let's get back to the book.

I'm Mad as Hell and I'm Not Going to Take it Anymore!

With that first assignment done, let's reflect on the success stories of your life.

A success story typically begins as a problem. You may have been bullied on the school playground. You may have lost your best friend. You might have been fired at a job. Whatever that problem was, many things happened to you in close proximity to that experience. And at some point, you emotionally screamed at the universe, "I'm mad as hell and I'm not going to take it anymore!" At that moment you made a decision and took definitive action. Things changed. Your problem went away and you walked away from that experience with a significant personal win in your life. Whether you know it or not, you just manifested change into your life. A celebration is in order! May I suggest a Rum Tiki drink?

We need to understand why and how those problems caused you to make the necessary decisions that changed your life. Replicating the general nature of those success experiences is what we need to expand upon today as we begin our journey to You 2.0. So, make sure you have a good 5-plus pages of emotionally charged problems, decisions, and actions in your journal. Emotionally stack those wins on top of each other. And once complete, stand back and look at your life's successes. What are you thinking? How do you feel? You should feel as though you just won the Super Bowl!

THE LIMITING BELIEF ASSIGNMENT

While you are in this creative Superman mode, let's document your belief system. What agreements have you made with yourself about what you can, cannot, and won't do. Again, we're not doing this to make you cast judgment on yourself, but to raise awareness of your conscious and subconscious minds regarding your thoughts, beliefs and actions.

Let's start with a few simple examples. "I can't lose weight because I'm big-boned; I would never drive a car from New York City to Orlando, Florida because it is too far; I won't fly in a small Cessna airplane because it is too dangerous. These are called "limiting beliefs." Others might call them emotional triggers that cause fear, paranoia, anxiety and procrastination.

It doesn't matter what you call them. If you think you can or cannot do something . . . anything, you're absolutely correct. And that is what you will attract into your life!

#	Limiting Belief	Why
1	ex. I can't start a business.	I don't have business training.
2	ex. I can't loose weight. I'm big-boned.	I've always been fat and never lost any weight.
3		
4		
5		

Figure 2

Whatever label gets put on them is ok for now. Just document what agreements you have with yourself about what you can't or won't do, and for what reason. Once again, we're not casting judgment. We're raising conscious awareness to what is going on in our minds. Shoot for at least 10 limiting beliefs. But if you really are in Superman mode, define them all.

And of course, once you have this activity complete, celebrate! Might I suggest a Rum Tiki drink? Hmmm. That's the second time I recommended that. Interesting!

You have just completed two critical introspective activities that have opened the door to the definition of your "You 1.0" self. I really want to congratulate you for completing these exercises. You have committed the act of introspection on yourself that many can't or won't even try to do. Just by these exercises alone, you have opened up a piece of your mind that is controlling you on a daily basis. Not an easy task. This change in awareness is causing you to grow. And personal growth needs celebration!

It's most likely a number of days later, so put everything into your three-ring binder, store it on the shelf, and let's get back into the book.

CHAPTER 2
HOW TO CHANGE YOUR THINKING

Before we put a blender inside your mind to change your thinking, I want to recommend you quickly acquire two additional books: the Dr. John Maxwell book, *"Becoming a Person of Influence,"* and a free PDF download of the Napoleon Hill book, *"Think and Grow Rich."* Both books supplement this book nicely when it comes to dealing with thinking in a different way.

Change Your Thinking to Change Your Results

Like it or not, we are bombarded daily with external stimuli that shapes our thinking, behaviors, actions, and results. Sprinkle in a few out-of-control emotions and we can find ourselves in a heap of trouble very fast.

Think a moment about where your training/programming came from historically, and where it comes from today: your parents, friends, neighbors, colleagues, church, grocery store, social media, Internet, and more. The sad fact about all this input is the sources don't remotely care about your "You 1.0" self, your "You 2.0" journey, your actions and beliefs or the results you are getting out of your life. And unfortunately, their historic training and programming is in control of your life. And if you're not getting what you need, want and desire out of your life, you need to remove, dare I say, "forget and unlearn" all of their influence and teachings from your head and reprogram yourself with beliefs and actions that will only positively enhance your "You 2.0 Self." The bottom line here is that we cannot live our lives by the training, teaching and opinion polls of others. STOP DOING IT!!!

And of course there is also the Rearview Mirror of Life! Except for the earlier "Introspection Assignments," we need to forget about yesterday and focus on increasing our awareness about thinking differently and how to do everything better, today and tomorrow. And to prove my point, I challenge anyone to drive from the East Coast to the West Coast, or vice versa, only using the rearview mirror. Yes. 3,000-4,000 miles only using the rearview mirror. Sounds kind of silly, right? Then I suggest you need to unlearn most everything from earlier in your life and relearn only those things that positively serve you on your journey to You 2.0!

With that, and moving on, hopefully we will all learn something new in this next section.

How the Conscious and Subconscious Minds Work

It was a time, long, long ago, (the early 1950s), in a land far, far away, (Texas), Dr. Thurman Fleet, a renowned chiropractor developed a conceptual model and therapy, Figure 3, where he explains how our "minds" work.

Figure 3 shows us that our Conscious "Thinking" Mind is the filter that lets things into your Subconscious "Emotional" Mind. And after years and years and years of input, whether for good or for bad, this all becomes your Belief System. And our Belief System drives our actions, which in turn creates our results.

So, if you aren't happy with your life's results, you need to change your actions and beliefs. And to change your actions and beliefs, you need to change the way you think, and the operational relationship between your Conscious "Thinking" mind and your Subconscious "Emotional" Mind.

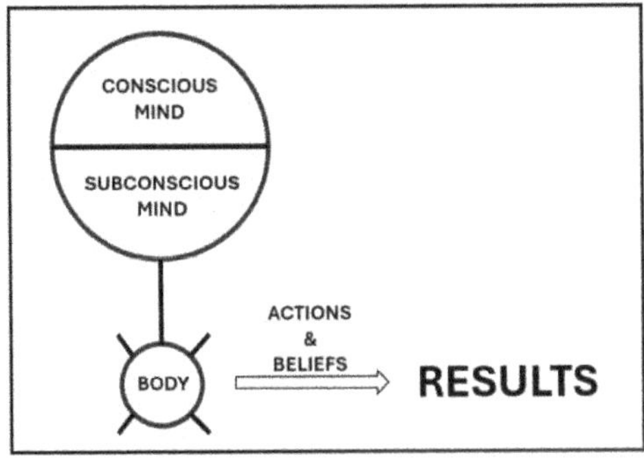

Figure 3

See? Easy Peezee! . . . Well, maybe not!

To help better set some context for a deeper dive that we'll now start, I need you to go back to the earliest days of your life.

Figure 4

In the Figure 4 diagram, you start life out as an unconscious, emotional being only. If something was wrong, or if you needed something, what did you do? You screamed and cried. Loudly and consistently! If your parents rectified the situation, you were happy and went silent. And the pattern repeated itself every handful of hours to your parent's disbelief!

By the way, as we peel back the various layers of the conscious and subconscious minds through these critical thinking exercises, be on the lookout for "patterns" in your thinking, actions, beliefs and results. If you can identify and increase your awareness to your conscious and subconscious mind's patterns, you can interrupt and delete those bad patterns, and enhance them with good, self-serving patterns in the future.

As you quickly approach the "Terrible Twos," I'm sure your parents have some other interesting stories about what you did on a daily basis. But what's important here is that you became a voracious and experiential sponge. You learned about everything in your environment. And how did you do that? You went mobile on the floor and put everything in your mouth. At this point in your life, you have no thinking or coping skills, but you quickly learned about your environment based on the feedback from your mouth.

Up until the approximate age of seven-or-so, you were the proverbial sponge. You took everything in; good, bad, ugly, right and wrong. Again, simply realize that you had no thinking or coping skills. You were in full discovery-acquisition mode.

However, somewhere around the age of seven or so, you begin the development of the conscious thinking mind. You have learned that by doing good things, there was positive feedback from your parents and your environment. And of course, if you did bad things, the parental and environmental feedback was not so positive. In a perfect world, you stayed on the positive side of life and your early memories are happy.

But at this time in life, you have limited knowledge and experience. So the journey to childhood wisdom begins.

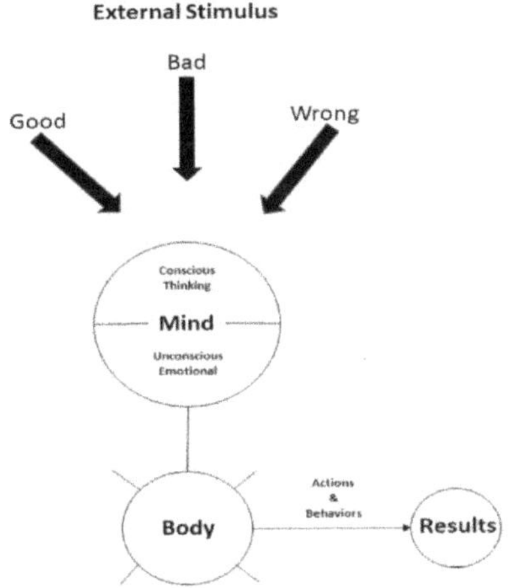

Figure 5

Think about this for a moment. As a child in Figure 5, you are fed external stimulus daily from everyone and everywhere around you. As a child you don't have the ability to filter what is directly coming into your unconscious, emotional mind. And your coping mechanism for all that input is the infamous "scream." Therefore, your actions, beliefs and results are fairly limited based on that input and those around you.

Now, flash forward to your high school days.

As a teenager, you have been fed stimuli for years and years and years. And that input has been good, bad, ugly, right and wrong. As a teen, you have a few more coping skills. Well, kind of! So your actions, behaviors and results are a bit more varied. But throw in a few squirts of out-of-control hormones and look out!!!

As you can see from the diagram, External Stimulus is constantly being introduced into our "conscious, logical mind." Our conscious mind filters that stimuli and passes some of it on to the subconscious, emotional mind that supports our current belief system, and that information gets assimilated into our being. Based on our programmed belief system, our physical body carries out a set of actions and behaviors that create the results that we get on a daily basis in our lives.

But what we need to understand is that the eternal stimulus continues to bombard us on a daily basis. On the job, out in the streets, with our friends, the parents. Influence is being exerted on us daily. And our beliefs and actions continue to modify.

At a certain age we would like to think that we would acquire wisdom, and life would be great from there on out. But it doesn't always work out that way. There's nothing more depressing than watching people walking around Disney World, heads-down and banging on their phones. What a waste! Sorry. I had to cast a bit of judgment there!

Flash forward a few years. You've now completed college, or trade school, or maybe dropped out of school altogether, and are living life on your own. Many days, you get the bear. On some "not so good days," the bear gets you! You get into a car accident, you lose your job, a family member dies. It could be one of many bad situations. And the programming you have received over the past many years takes center stage and your beliefs and actions drive the day. If your programming and belief system is in reasonable shape, your results will be reasonable. If not, your results could be tragic.

This is why our Introspection Assignment from earlier is so critically important. The "good" inside of us will control our actions and results. But also know, the "bad" inside of us will control us as well.

We might have learned a critical life lesson as a teenager, but we need to ask ourselves the big question, "does a lesson learned back then serve me today in this situation, 30 years later?" If the answer is yes, and it truly serves you, then take the appropriate action. If that lesson doesn't serve you in the situation today, stop immediately. You cannot implement that decision and those actions from your historic programming from years ago. Don't look now, but you're acquiring wisdom!

So what we need to be critically aware of is that the thinking of many years ago will not serve us today. Therefore, our thinking needs to change. The tragic flaw here is that we usually will implement the thinking from years ago and not get the result we want today. We get frustrated and walk away angry. Well, two years later, almost the same situation recurs. We make the same decision based on thinking from years ago and end up again with a bad result. Again, we end up angry and frustrated. If this situation recurs again and again and again, and we use the same thinking, we will always get the same, bad or wrong result. Essentially, we learn nothing from our environmental stimulus.

Albert Einstein once said, "The definition of insanity is doing the same thing over and over again, expecting a different result."

Think about it. Is it reasonable that the thinking and behaviors of a teenager 30 years ago properly serve an adult today? Most likely not. And again, if you're not happy with the results you are getting in your life today, maybe your thinking is not in order and needs to be changed so it properly serves you today, and into the future.

So when would "now" be a good time to take a deeper dive and learn more about our thinking process?

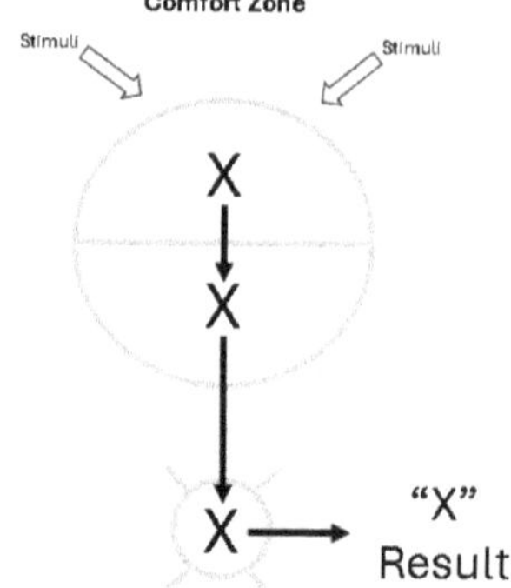

Figure 6

As we look closer at Figure 6, we see that external stimuli that we seek migrates towards "X." Maybe we're focused on input for "X confirmation bias." Our daily focus on "X" makes it to our subconscious mind and becomes our belief system. We take the appropriate "X" action and get an appropriate "X" result, and life is good. Woo-hoo!

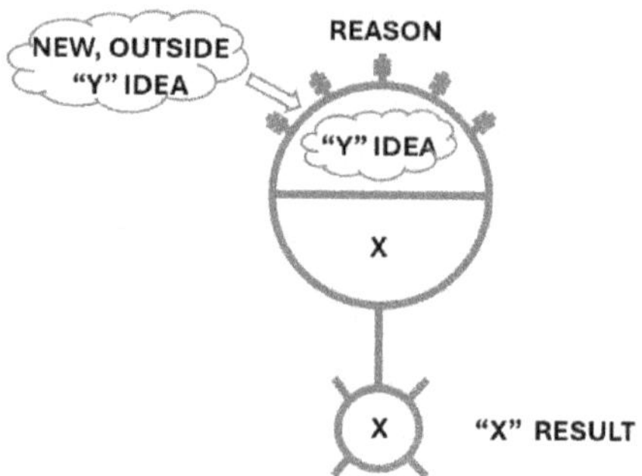

Figure 7

BUT!!!

Why is there always a "but?"

In a worst case scenario, it is Friday afternoon. You're starting to wind down for a long weekend, and a new, outside, unknown "Y idea" makes it into your conscious awareness. You were so focused on the beach and ocean, and the "Y idea" breaches your consciousness. DAMN!!!

Of course, your conscious, thinking mind passes "Y" on to the subconscious mind, and the storm begins. The new "Y" belief is in direct conflict with your old "X" belief system.

The new Y idea, "I need move to another state for my job" is in direct conflict with the X belief, "I only work 40 hours a week." The storm continues to grow in your subconscious mind and you need to make a decision and take action. All you can think about is the Wizard of Oz, and mentally, "it's a twister, it's a twister!!!" as you spin in circles. Fear, paranoia, procrastination and a few other bad things come to roost in your conscious mind. The beach safe haven and long weekend is gone.

Your X beliefs will reign supreme, and 40 hours a week it is. Equilibrium is restored. A new life at Virginia Beach would be a new start. More money. More responsibility. MORE WORK!!! But if I stay right here in my X lifestyle, no change, no additional money, no additional work. Just comfort. . .DONE!!!

If you have played life easy and comfortable, you'll most likely take the easy way out. It's easy, yes. But if you want more out of life, frustrating!

So now you're standing at the doorway of the Terror Barrier. What do you do? What decision do you make? Look no further than your belief system and you'll have your answer.

The bottom line here is that the way you think, believe and act in the here and now is representative of your life results. So, if you're not happy with the results you are getting in your daily life, you need to change your decisions, actions and behaviors. And to change your decisions, actions and behaviors, you need to change the way you think.

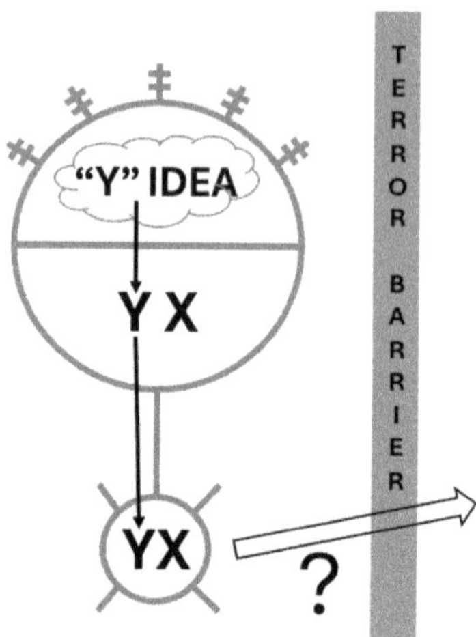

Figure 8

The bottom line question: "When your input, belief system, actions and behaviors have you strolling up to the Terror Barrier, figure 8 what decision will you make?"

Simple! Well, maybe not so simple.

You will need to seriously assess whether the decision you are about to make serves the programming and you of yesterday, possibly 30 years ago, or will the decision serve the you of tomorrow on your You 2.0 Journey?

Let's return to our Introspection Mode Assignment from earlier and ask our subconscious and emotional mind, "are our actions and beliefs serving us appropriately and are the results representative of what we are expecting out of our life at this moment in time?"

If the answer is "yes," then congratulations. You are most likely on track to achieving your purpose in life. If the answer is "no," then it is a good thing you have this book in your hands at this time in your life.

If that answer is no, and you aren't getting the results you want or expect out of your life, then we need to assess who is providing us with input that we are acting upon. I'm guessing that some people should never, ever be giving you counsel on anything. Do yourself a favor and limit or remove/delete their input.

Rechaud

Just to illustrate this point with a specific example, Tony Robbins tells a story about Rechaud, a medically confirmed stutterer. His wife took him to many doctors and speech therapists, and nobody could help.

One day Tony received a communication from Rechaud's wife explaining the situation. And of course, in true Tony fashion, Rechaud ended up standing directly in front of Tony.

As Rechaud relives the story, Rechaud's father was quite the abusive husband. And one day, in an attempt to stop the abuse, Rechaud started to stutter. Thinking that something was medically wrong, the abuse stopped immediately, and all loving focus was put on Rechaud. As long as there was stuttering in the environment, so was there peace. Interesting solution thinking for a two-year-old, huh?

But it's now thirty years later, and that stuttering solution has negatively impacted Rechaud's life in many, many ways. He struggled and failed in college and couldn't maintain a job because of his inability to properly communicate with others.

Did the lesson learned from thirty years ago solve a significant issue? Of course it did! Does that lesson learned serve a thirty year old Rechaud in the here and now? Absolutely not!

Tony took Rechaud back to that point in time and when Rechaud realized his stuttering solution after watching a Rocky and Bullwinkle cartoon when Bullwinkle called to Rocky for help, at which time Rechaud made his stuttering cry for help. And peace fell over the kingdom!

Unfortunately, it became a pattern that stayed in place for thirty years. But after a seven minute intervention with Tony, Rechaud's stuttering stopped forever. And he was able to communicate with no issues!

If I said this once, I've said it thousands of times: "The Mind can be a terrible thing!"

And that's why we're here today. To fix your thinking, fix your belief system, fix your behaviors and actions, and ultimately, change your life's results

.You may not be a stutterer, but in your Limiting Belief exercise, is there something in your past that is negatively impacting you in the here and now? If you tell me "no," and your life is a mess, I'll tell you to think harder!

This is clearly a case for having the best, brightest and most helpful people in your life. For those that are providing valuable input to your successful current and future actions, behaviors and results, seek them out for more input. Or go find others like them to enhance what is going successfully in your life. Ah hah, enter stage left the concept of your Mastermind! Again, the topic for another book.

THE INFLUENCE ASSIGNMENT

Go back to your quiet space and start defining everyone that holds a place of influence in your life. And I mean everyone!

Once you have everyone named on paper, in a second column, identify if they are a positive influence on your actions, behaviors and results, or are they a negative impact? In a third column, add the details of "how" they are a positive, negative, or neutral influence in your life. This will be a difficult task to perform, and it will take an unemotionally brutal and honest assessment. But those that aren't accepting and actively involved with your journey to You 2.0, do yourself a favor and restrict their input to your journey.

As you arrive to this part of the book, you now have a clear definition of your You 1.0. Your Introspection Assignment should have opened your eyes as to the why and how you got to where you are right now.

You understand all the good decisions you've made across time in both your personal and professional lives. It is a combination of all these decisions, actions and behaviors that need to be emotionally enhanced and taken forward with you on your "You 2.0 Journey."

You have a good handle on all of your historic limiting beliefs that are currently driving your belief system. Remember, they're limiting beliefs for a reason. Make sure you delete them from your entire being and thought processes and create a belief system that has empowering beliefs that enhance you as a person and serves you well on the journey to You 2.0.

We spent some time discussing our "Thinking/Emotional Minds," and how they were programmed, and what you need to do to change your results, getting what you want out of life.

And finally, we talked about those people in your sphere of influence. And whether they are supportive in your personal and professional lives, and if their influence serves you or sabotages you. This exercise and understanding will definitely provide the most anxiety to your mental state. So please be sure of the decisions you make here.

At this point you have everything documented from history you need to sail off on your You 2.0 Journey. You have everything you need to be successful. It is now, all up to you!

At this point some people would tell you, "good luck!" But getting and/or having good luck is only an emotional concept for the wholly unprepared. If you did all of the exercises to the best of your abilities, you have everything you need to be successful. And luck is not a factor. The only thing left now is, "Implementation!"

With complete readiness at hand . . .

GO!!!

CHAPTER 3
DEFINING YOU 2.0

First off, congratulations on making it this far. You most likely have found out a lot about yourself. Some of it good, some of it not so good, and some of it, well, run away like your hair is on fire!

Any change, no matter how big or small needs to begin with a definition of where you are today. Your starting point isn't good, bad or ugly. It is simply your starting point. What you have done to date in your life is only informational in nature and somewhat immaterial. What you do from here forward is critical to your journey to You 2.0

Defining the You 2.0 of Tomorrow

At this point you have a good understanding of who you are, and what got you to where you are in life today. Again, don't think of it as good, bad or ugly. Think of it as only your starting point.

Shortly we'll begin defining what your You 2.0 looks like. But before we put pen to paper, or fingers to keyboard, we need to talk about your core values and interests. They are critical to the definition of You 2.0.

Core values and interests are the fundamental beliefs and principles that guide your decisions, actions, and overall life. Depending on your historic programming, your values and interests may need to be tweaked a bit. Maybe significantly! We need to be sure we have a clearly defined set of values and interests that will help us navigate through our upcoming journey as we work to achieve our future and successful You 2.0 self.

To set a bit of context, core values and interests are important because they provide a framework that will help you make the best decisions that properly serve you in the here and now. This framework will create a flexible attitude to help you get through troubling challenges and setbacks. It will help you create and manage relationships that are essential for your journey. You will be an honest, self-aware, compassionate person with integrity, respect, courage and gratitude.

Identifying your core values and interests is a valuable exercise. It involves introspection, reflection, and sometimes seeking counsel from others. Once you've identified your core values and interests, you can use them to align your goals, make informed decisions, and live a more purposeful and fulfilling life.

DEFINING THE YOU 2.0 ASSIGNMENT

The next step in the process has to do with your You 2.0 vision. We need to send you back into your quiet space again for more introspection. This time it is all about where you want to go and what you want to do and accomplish in your upcoming and new future you. Let's start this section and assignment off with a notable quote from Walt Disney. "If you can dream it, you can achieve it!"

Vision Strategy Execution – VSE

The plan you are going to create will be no different than waking up on any given Friday and planning a vacation from Chicago to Miami Beach. Do you want to drive, fly, take the bus or train? Maybe you need to stop over in Nashville and Atlanta. This could get complicated quickly. Creating the journey from You 1.0 to You 2.0 will be just as interesting. Fortunately, you have this book in your hands, so no worries! And you are about to learn about your You 2.0 VSE Transition Plan.

VSE is a simple acronym for Vision Strategy Execution.

Vision is the definition of your You 2.0 end goal. Strategy is the high-level set of goals that will guide your journey. And Execution represents the very specific steps you need to perform on a daily, weekly or monthly basis to complete your strategies and achieve your vision.

So let's take a closer look at the VSE Tool.

The Vision Strategy Execution Tool

Notice how the Vision flows down into five strategic goals. And the five goals flow down to a number of very specific action steps to take. So if you implement the twelve specific Execution Tasks, you will complete the five strategies, and ultimately achieve your You 2.0 Vision.

Just know that your specific vision might have seven or eight strategies and maybe fifteen or twenty execution tasks. Or maybe four strategic goals and ten tasks. Your specific vision will drive the necessary number of Strategies and Execution Tasks. This tool isn't about how many items you document. It is about the number of strategic categories and the necessary action steps to take to meet your vision.

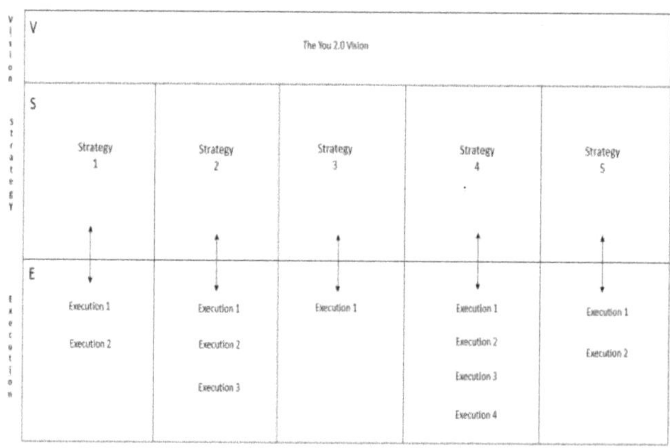

Figure 9

The VSE in Action

One of my clients told me they wanted to become a project manager in Hawaii. Each component of that vision, becoming a project manager and restarting life in Hawaii are two different goals that just don't happen overnight. If you are not a project manager today, it is most likely a two-to-three year set of tasks to get to that certification/job. Moving to Hawaii? Unless someone is paying to move you there, it may be a 6-month to a year activity to make that happen. Do you see why this journey requires your focus and flexibility?

So what does a VSE look like in this specific example?

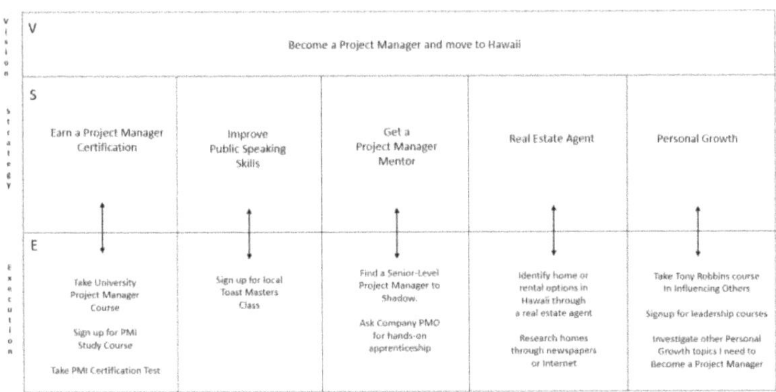

Figure 10

As a rule of thumb, consider the Execution tasks as what needs to happen in the next six months-to-two years. The strategic goals, maybe two-to-four years. And because your strategies may change over the coming years, it may take four-to-five years to achieve your vision. Again, your gas mileage may differ!

So there you have it. The details behind creating a VSE.

CREATING THE VSE ASSIGNMENT

Now, as you take pen to paper, or fingers to keyboard, simply create the "end state" of what your You 2.0 looks like in your mind. Create the vision of what you are doing every day, where do you go, who are you talking to, what are you driving, what you are eating, where are you vacationing, what kind of home are you living in, what do you smell, see, etc. You need to totally immerse and fully integrate yourself into your complete and finished You 2.0 vision. Put simply, you need to be using your imagination to actually be living in your future life. Right now! Everyday! It must be palpable!

Now. Put this book down and define your You 2.0 in as much detail as possible on paper. Do not skip anything! Documenting your vision and setting up your VSE will take time, so please don't rush your creative process. You might even want to go to YouTube and do a search on Spiritual Creativity Music to play in the background while you are writing.

Transitioning Your "You 2.0 Vision" to Your VSE

It is most likely a few days later, and now that you have a complete and detailed list of everything involved in your new You 2.0 life, we need to identify the necessary Strategies and Tasks and get all of those details into your "You 2.0 VSE."

This too will take a few days with some serious introspection, some consultation with people in your circle of influence, and a number of rewrites. Getting the Strategies and Tasks as close to finalized is critical. Take your time and get it right!

So bookmark this page and we'll continue this discussion in a few days.

The You 1.0-to-You 2.0 Gap to Close

WOW!!! You have achieved another major achievement on your journey to You 2.0. You have achieved the definition of your You 1.0 self, where you are today, and the definition of your You 2.0 self, where you want/need to be tomorrow. You have taken all of the future data and now have it populated in your VSE.

I would highly recommend going back to your stationary store and buy a large white board and markers of many colors. This will become the vision board of your upcoming journey.

On the left side of your vision board, define your You 1.0 self. On the right side, your You 2.0 self. In the middle of the white board, write, "You 2.0 Journey Gap to Close!"

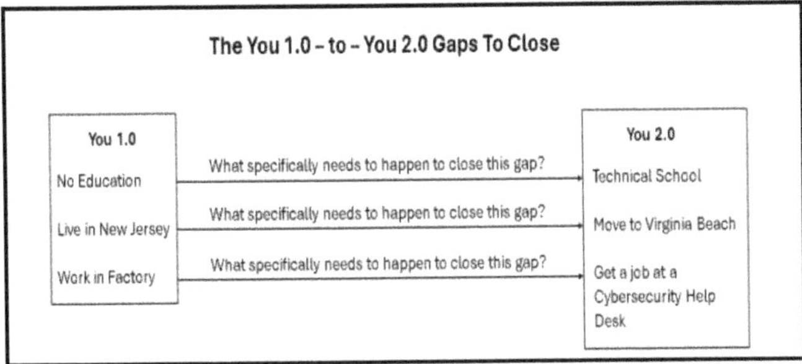

Figure 11

While this is a simple example, your list of today's You 1.0 and tomorrow's You 2.0 will be significantly different. But what is critically important is mapping those things that need to change from today-to-tomorrow, including a list of seven or so things that need to happen to make the transition successful. Again, your list and mileage will differ!

Journal Your Experiences

Earlier we talked about tools necessary to document your journey. It is important that this documentation is free of emotions and only discusses "the facts!" Done properly, this documentation is quite sterile. And it needs to be to track and monitor your progress. And if something goes drastically wrong, sterile facts will make troubleshooting issues much easier.

At the same time, you are not a sterile person. You are a tragically flawed, emotional human being. So I am going to recommend that you journal this experience.

Journaling is a personal practice that involves writing down your thoughts, feelings, experiences, and reflections. It is a way to explore your inner thoughts, assess emotions, and gain insights into your journey.

Remember, journaling is a personal practice. There is no right or wrong way to do it. The most important thing is to find a method that works for you, and write, write, write!!!

CHAPTER 4
THE YOU 2.0
IMPLEMENTATION CHANGE
PROCESS

Now that you are at the You 2.0 Implementation Process, you're probably saying to yourself, "this is going to be a lot of work!"

Well, yes. This is going to be a lot of work. But fear not. This book is the "Definitive Owner's Manual to Changing Your Life!" And I'm not going to throw you into the deep end of the pool without some meaningful, "How To" help.

In the software development world where I project managed R&D efforts for well over 20 years, we have something called "The Change Management Process." This is simply a structured approach to transition teams and organizations from an "As Is" state, where you are today, to a "To Be" state, where you want to be tomorrow. The process is simply:

- Initiation
- Planning
- Execution
- Evaluation
- Closure

Let's take a semi-deeper look into each of these steps.

Initiation

Why is the change necessary and how does it align with your future goals. Hopefully you have a mentor, coach, and/or others to assist as your change management team as you work your way through the change process.

Planning

Analyze your current state (You 1.0), and identify the desired future state, (You 2.0). This is where your VSE comes into play and help define what will be happening over the coming months/years. If you were in Corporate America, you would be reporting on the progress of your change effort, so I'll ask you to do the same thing. You need to be reporting to someone on the status of your change effort. It can be your wife, husband, mentor, neighbor, whoever.

Execution

Now that you have planned the work, it's time to work the plan. What ever you need to do to implement the tasks on your VSE, do them. Do you have the necessary skills and knowledge? If yes, start running as fast as you can. If no, figure out how to get the necessary skills and knowledge to get your You 2.0 Journey underway. And of course, track your progress and tell others about what you are doing and going through.

Evaluation

This is where we evaluate or test the end result of our tasks to make sure we successfully complete any activities to achieve a specific strategy in our VSE. If progress is steady and consistent, stay the course. But if things aren't proceeding as planned, changes will be necessary, and most likely there will be challenges to overcome.

Closure

This is the final step in the overall change process where you acknowledge arrival at the You 2.0 destination and end the journey. My recommendation here would be something more significant than previous recommendations. Like, a two-week vacation to Hawaii. Maybe Paris, France. Japan. It must be spectacular! And if you're young enough, there might be a You 3.0 Journey in your future. So be sure to journal the process, document best practices and lessons learned. Worst case scenario, you have tons of documentation for your autobiography.

This is the structured approach to managing your journey. This process works no matter if you are building a piece of software, a boat, an airplane, a rocket ship, or simply creating a new you. If you don't follow this structured approach, it is reasonable to assume you will be met with chaos and frustration.

But as we acknowledged earlier, this is a lot of work. So to be successful, work with your wife, husband, children, neighbor, lawyer. Whoever is going on this journey with you. If you build a good working relationship with what we call your stakeholders, the chances of achieving You 2.0 are exponentially higher. Be sure to expect and mitigate problems and resistance along the way. If there are any questions, comments or concerns along the way, deal with them immediately.

While this change plan comes from a software development environment, it will work for you to monitor and control your journey and achieve your desired outcomes.

Creating the Transition Plan

Now that you have a feel for the change process and what you need to do, and now that you have defined your starting point, You 1.0, and your finishing point, You 2.0, now the fun begins. Creating a plan that will actually get from your starting point to your finishing point.

You have your overarching vision of where you want to be. You have a number of strategies that form the basis of achieving that vision. And you have a list of tactical action steps to perform over the coming months. But what do you do first?

While the entire plan is important to achieving your vision, you need to prioritize the list of tasks. And just like in Corporate America, achieving early wins is very important. It sets the context and tone for what is about to come. It's also critically important to achieve early wins. They set momentum. As you prioritize these tasks, determine a few that can be completed quickly.

Signing up for a Toastmasters Speaking class that meets once weekly is an easy and early win. Look for a few wins such as this to get your journey moving. You probably need to sign up for a class at your local university or vocational tech school. If you can achieve a number of tasks while in night school to develop a new knowledgebase or skill, momentum will build and you will get excited to keep the journey going.

If you are currently working a full time job, you can't get too many of your tasks in flight at the same time. In the realm of project management, we strive for an 80% - 85% productivity rate. We assume that we will be busy up to 85% of the time. Of course you'll ask, "well what about the remaining 15%? Good question!

You might be aware of our good friend Murphy and his wonderful Law: *If something can go wrong, it will.* And those emergencies will consume at least 15% of your time, if not more. So for the first month or two, try to restrict your personal and professional lives to 60 – 65 hours a week. Maximum. There will be weeks you will work longer. And there will be weeks you work less. Anything that takes you over 60 hours a week needs to be an issue of such critical importance that it threatens the plan you are implementing.

And if you are working a full time job, try to limit your evening journey tasks to 2 hours each night. Dying on your You 2.0 Journey due to an 80+ hour work week is unacceptable and should be avoided at all costs!

So you have your tasks, you have your plan. Take the plan to a few extremely helpful friends and make sure your plan is doable. If you know someone that is a project manager, go to them for assistance. We have a unique understanding of how projects need to be implemented. A project manager could be your best accountability partner!

Implementing Your "You 2.0" Plan

The good news is that you now have a plan to guide you on your You 2.0 journey. However, you need to understand that a change journey is almost never a straight line from start to finish. Can you travel on a straight line from Chicago to Miami Beach. Of course not. There is not one road that can make it happen if you were to drive, bus or train there. Even if you fly, you may be able to do a direct flight to Miami, but you'll need a car, bus or Uber to take you from the airport to Miami Beach. The same goes for your You 2.0 journey. While there is no straight line to your destination, you can at least make sure you are directionally correct. So what does "directionally correct" mean?

Your "You 2.0" Plan is designed to act as a set of guardrails around you on the journey for your safety. No different than a pair of guardrails on both side of a road. If you stay within these guardrails, you will remain directionally correct. The following graphic is a perfect example.

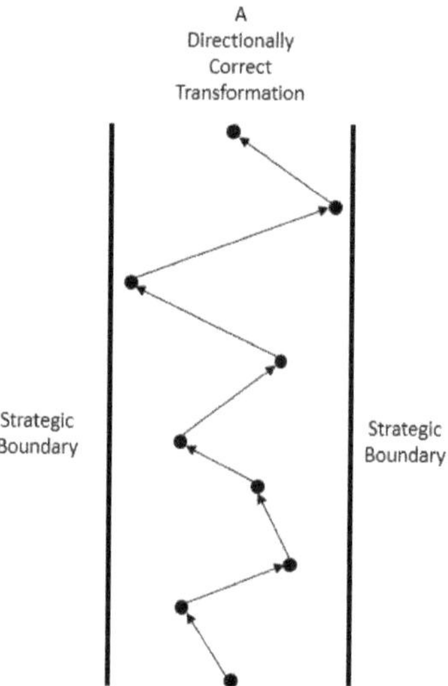

Figure 12

Your journey will surely get you to start and stop along the way. Turn left and turn right. As long as you are moving forward and stay within the guardrails, you will be directionally correct on your journey to the You 2.0 destination. This is the "goal."

Well that certainly seems intuitive. But again, what about the infamous Murphy's Law. If something can go wrong, it will go wrong. And you will no longer be directionally correct. Now what do we do?

Let's start by looking at what "Not directionally Correct" looks like. The graphic below shows just what that means.

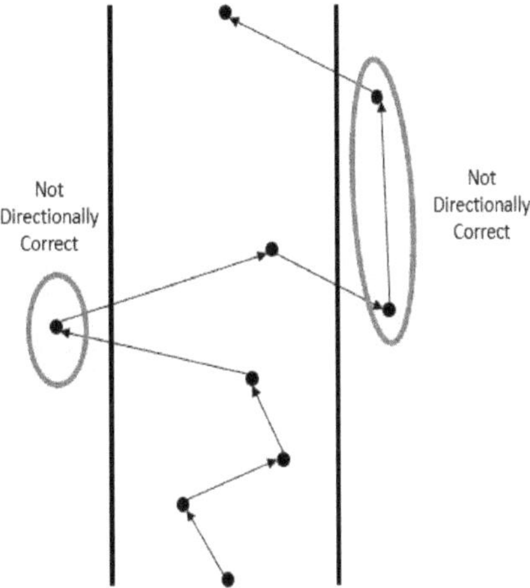

Figure 13

In this graphic we see two times we wandered outside of our You 2.0 guardrails. In either case, only bad things can happen. And achieving You 2.0 status will become delayed for a period of time.

But take a closer look at this graphic. Not only did we lose track of our guardrails, on the right side we even went backwards. And yet our next step was still outside of the guardrails.

If you are to find this happening, you need to go back and review your Execution tasks. Maybe you documented a necessary task incorrectly. Maybe you misinterpreted that task to perform. No matter why you are outside of your safety guardrails, immediate action is necessary to get back into a state of "directionally correct." And by the way, a good project will see this jumping of the guardrails weeks, if not months in advance. Seeing into the future and assessing issues and risks is a critical skill we have. Seek out your project manager if you wander into this situation.

To stop you from getting lost on your You 2.0 Journey, it would be a very wise recommendation to sit down quarterly and review your overall plan and action steps. If you find a problem three months into an eighteen-month task, resolution should be easy and quick.

However, if you're not paying attention and you come up on month seventeen and you just now find a problem, getting out of this problem could be a lengthy and costly process. Do yourself a favor and do a quarterly and year-end review. This is your greatest advantage at making sure your plan will stay on track.

Measuring Task Success Against Goals

If you have ever been to business school or attended a personal growth seminar, you learned it is important to effectively measure task success against your established strategies and vision. It is essential to have a measurable framework. Here are some key strategies to consider:

- Define SMART Goals
- Create a Tracking System, Monitor and Report Progress
- Use your team to assess progress and feedback
- Celebrate achievements
- Learn from Failures
- Continuously evaluate and adjust

Define Clear and Measurable Goals

If you have ever read about or engaged in personal development, you have read about SMART Goals. SMART Goals are Specific, Measurable, Achievable, Relevant, and Time-bound. They are neatly wrapped in what are called Key Performance Indicators, or KPIs. They are specific metrics that will indicate progress regarding each task and strategy.

Create a Tracking System, Monitor and Report Progress

In a software development project, Corporate America uses many tools to monitor, track and report on projects. If you're going to be spending ten million dollars on a project, it needs to be monitored and closely controlled. Your You 2.0 Journey is going to be worth a couple of million dollars over the next five-to-ten years, so let's follow Corporate Americas lead.

While Corporate America has reasonably deep financial pockets, very specific and technology-dependent tools are used. Actually, you're in luck! Everything you need to be doing as defined in this book can be done with a spreadsheet, word document, power point presentation, calendaring, and video collaboration tools. Everything you need is in an off the shelf, office suite of tools, or available as a free, open-source office suite. Either will work. Track and monitor your progress consistently and report your progress on a quarterly basis at a minimum.

Create Feedback Mechanisms

Because this is your personal journey, your self-assessment along the way is critical. Why? Because it is your journey and you know where you need to go and what you need to do. But be careful. Hopefully you created a team to assist you on the journey. As they aren't as emotionally attached to your journey, they are more able to see a "forest view" of they journey. Because you are emotionally tangled up in the journey, your view could be one of, "picking weeds at the base of a tree, and not able to see the bigger picture, forest view of the journey." Seek advice and counsel from others to make sure others see the same "facts" as you.

Celebrate Achievements

Earlier in the book we celebrated a few achievements with a Rum Tiki Drink. The goal is to celebrate achievements. Do whatever you feel is appropriate. But most importantly, celebrate those achievements, milestones and goals. These celebrations will serve as driving motivation, momentum, and positive reinforcement to keep your journey on track.

Learn from Failures

While taking the time to learn from failures appears somewhat counter-intuitive, taking the time to analyze failures and setbacks is a critical learning mechanism. If you understand the reasons for setbacks and failures, you will learn from them, never make the same mistake again, and never become an Albert Einstein "insanity" statistic.

But more importantly, learning from these setbacks requires a re-review of your plan and approach. Your strategies could be semi-flawed. And by making changes to your plan in real time, you can guarantee that you won't make similar mistakes in the future.

Continuously Evaluate and Adjust

This is probably the most important step at managing the success of your efforts going forward.

When you created the plan and started implementing it long ago, you performed planning with semi-perfect information. And as any project moves forward through its lifecycle, things change; for good and for bad.

As project managers, we never want to get nine months into a ten month effort and bump into an "oops" that will set our efforts back seven months. Similarly, you need to be evaluating your efforts on at least a quarterly and year-end basis to make sure your plan is moving forward appropriately and successfully. Depending on the timeline of your efforts, a formal, monthly review might be very informative and appropriate. Most importantly, you need to be flexible and adjust your approach and timeline if/as needed.

By following these steps, you can effectively measure task success against your established goals and ensure that you're on track to achieve your desired outcomes.

Leadership and Dr. John Maxwell

To this point in the book, what you have been asked to do is very tactical regarding the steps on your You 2.0 Journey. However, there is a required strategic component to the journey as well. Hence the "S" in your VSE!

I would like to take a moment to introduce everyone reading this book, my coach and teacher, Dr. John Maxwell. He has written many, many books on the topic of leadership. In fact, as it turns out, I am also a certified John Maxwell Coach, Speaker and Trainer.

If you know of Dr. John, you know of what I speak. If you don't know of him, I suggest you immediately get a copy of his book, *Becoming a Person of Influence.*

Additionally, his books represent a wealth of knowledge regarding what successful leadership looks like and what needs to happen on a daily basis. Do yourself a favor and create a John Maxwell Library. In addition to the book listed above, I would also recommend you get: *The 21 Irrefutable Laws of Leadership, Developing the Leader Within You 2.0, and Everyone Communicates, Few Connect.* By the time you figure out how to assimilate these four books into your subconscious mind and life, you will become a fan of Maxwell.

The journey you are currently on cannot be done only by yourself in a vacuum. You need support from others along the way. Needing others represents leadership. And leadership represents influencing others. And influencing others is a necessary skill to learn. Not only for this particular journey, but for every other day in your life as well.

So I'd like to take a moment to introduce you to a few bits of wisdom from John Maxwell that will be very helpful as you proceed on this journey, and through the rest of your life. They are relationships and accountability.

Build Working Relationships

Intentional Relationships

Maxwell emphasizes the importance of being intentional in your relationships. This means actively investing time, energy, and effort into building and nurturing connections. By being intentional, you can create deeper, more meaningful relationships.

Servant Leadership

Maxwell's concept of servant leadership involves putting the needs of others before your own. When you focus on serving others, you create a positive and supportive environment that fosters strong relationships.

Adding Value to Others

Maxwell believes that the best way to build relationships is to add value to the lives of others. This can involve offering support, encouragement, or simply being a good listener. By adding value, you demonstrate that you care about the other person and their well-being.

Trust and Integrity

Building trust is essential for strong relationships. Maxwell emphasizes the importance of being honest, reliable, and trustworthy. By demonstrating integrity, you create a foundation of trust that can support a deep and lasting relationship.

Communication

Effective communication is crucial for building and maintaining relationships. Maxwell stresses the importance of active listening, clear communication, and empathy. By practicing effective communication, you can build stronger connections with others.

Influence

Maxwell's leadership framework also includes the concept of influence. By understanding how to influence others positively, you can create stronger relationships and motivate others to achieve their goals.

Accountability Partners

Choose the Right Partner

- Shared Goals: Look for someone who shares your goals and values.
- Mutual Respect: Ensure there's a foundation of trust and respect between you.
- Commitment: Both partners should be committed to the accountability relationship.

Define Clear Expectations

- Roles and Responsibilities: Clearly outline each partner's role in the relationship.
- Frequency of Check-ins: Determine how often you'll meet or communicate.
- Feedback Mechanism: Establish a process for providing feedback and support.

Build Trust and Accountability

- Honesty and Transparency: Be open and honest about your progress and challenges.
- Support and Encouragement: Offer support and encouragement to your partner.
- Follow Through: Hold yourself and your partner accountable for commitments.

Provide Constructive Feedback

- Specific and Actionable: Give feedback that is specific, actionable, and helpful.
- Focus on Improvement: Aim to help your partner grow and develop.
- Avoid Judgment: Be supportive and avoid blaming or shaming.

Celebrate Successes

- Acknowledge Achievements: Recognize and celebrate each other's successes.
- Positive Reinforcement: Provide encouragement and motivation.

Address Challenges

- Open Communication: Discuss challenges openly and honestly.
- Problem-Solving: Work together to find solutions and overcome obstacles.
- Adjustments: Be willing to adjust your approach as needed.

By implementing these principles in your life, you can create deeper, more meaningful relationships with the people in your life and create strong and effective accountability partnerships that will help you achieve your You 2.0 goals and for whatever journeys throughout the rest of your life.

CHAPTER 5
YOU 2.0 LESSONS LEARNED AND NEXT STEPS

Lessons Learned

Earlier in this book we considered a quote from Albert Einstein who said, "the definition of insanity is doing the same thing over and over again and expecting a different result!" From my perspective, that does sound a bit crazy. And something we should all strive to never, ever do. And that's where the concept of Lessons Learned comes into play.

Lessons learned are just that. Something good, bad or ugly happened that we weren't expecting or planned for. We needed to depart from the plan and make changes. It could cost days, weeks or even months. For whatever reason. And we need to document those lessons so if they happen again in the future, we don't make the same mistakes again. Ahh, learning from your mistakes. What a novel approach to acquiring wisdom and success! Just be sure to document everything. If you thoroughly document all of your lessons with the reasoning behind them, you have committed the act or personal development and growth. Something that will pay off later in your career and life. Don't forget. We run on patterns. What happens in our professional lives will happen in our personal lives. And vice versa. Don't get caught performing an act of badness in your personal life, just because you didn't learn a lesson about people in your professional life.

Learning Needs To Be Fun!

Approaching and Implementing Lifelong Learning

Lifelong learning is a commitment to continuous growth and development. It involves actively seeking out new knowledge and skills throughout your life. Here are some strategies to help you approach and implement lifelong learning:

Identify Your Learning Goals

- **Reflect on your interests:** What topics or subjects intrigue you?

- **Consider your career:** Are there specific skills or knowledge that would benefit your professional development?

- **Personal growth:** What areas of your personal life do you want to improve?

Create a Learning Plan

Set realistic goals: Break down your learning goals into smaller, achievable steps.

Allocate time: Schedule regular time for learning activities.

Choose your resources: Determine the best resources for your learning style, such as books, online courses, workshops, or mentors.

Embrace a Growth Mindset

Challenge yourself: Step outside of your comfort zone and try new things.

View failures as learning opportunities: Learn from your mistakes and use them as stepping stones for growth.

Celebrate your progress: Acknowledge and reward your achievements, no matter how small.

Find a Learning Community

Connect with like-minded individuals: Join groups, clubs, or online communities that share your interests.

Learn from others: Exchange ideas, collaborate on projects, and seek guidance from mentors.

Utilize Technology

Online courses: Platforms like Coursera, edX, and Udemy offer a wide range of courses on various subjects.

Podcasts: Listen to podcasts on topics that interest you while commuting or doing chores.

Apps: Use educational apps to learn new skills or practice existing ones.

Make Learning Fun

Choose enjoyable activities: Engage in learning activities that you find interesting and enjoyable.

Mix it up: Try different learning methods to keep things fresh.

Reflect and Evaluate

Track your progress: Keep a journal or use a learning management system to monitor your progress.

Evaluate your learning: Reflect on what you've learned and how it's impacted your life.

By following these strategies, you can make lifelong learning a rewarding and fulfilling part of your journey. Remember, the most important thing is to stay curious, motivated, and committed to continuous growth.

The Plan and Next Steps

1) Be sure to read and re-read the book from cover to cover. Do all of the exercises and start your journey.

2) Make the Plan, then work the Plan. Adjust tactically and strategically if/as necessary. Quickly! Get momentum and do whatever is necessary to keep it!

3) Once you are working the Plan, check back in with the book monthly to make sure you are following the process. This is one journey you don't want to be making any mistakes. Keep working the Plan until you reach your You 2.0 finish line. Never stop!

You have almost reached the end of this book. And if you're anything like me, you are probably here after a quick scan to better understand what you are being asked to do. And if this is you too, that's ok. You now need to go back to the very beginning of the book and carefully read each and every page. Write notes in the margins that help you critically move the needle on your journey. In fact, get a few different color highlighters to mark concept that are critical or important. More important, get to Section 1 and do *The Introspection Assignment.* It's time to get this journey moving forward. And there is no more important than doing these activities.

Be sure you completely understand the section on how the conscious and subconscious minds work. After all, this book is all about changing the way you think. You cannot reach You 2.0 with your current You 1.0 thinking!

Make sure you have a solid definition of your You 1.0, your You 2.0, and the gaps to close to move from one version of you to the other.

Of course, make the plan, then work the plan. And do not stop until you arrive at your You 2.0 detailed definition you created through the various tasks in this book.

And of course, once you cross the threshold of the You 2.0 Journey, celebrate, celebrate, celebrate!!! After all, you just completed a major change in your life. No go out and enjoy it!

EPILOGUE

Now that you have really reached the end of the book and crossed the finish line to You 2.0, I want to congratulate you on a job very well done. It's most likely you have been on this journey for many months, if not a few years.

But!!!

There's that "but" again. DAMN!!!

While the good news is that you have achieved You 2.0, the somewhat better news is that the journey doesn't end here.

You are at a new place, in a new life, with a new you! You will know within the first year at this destination if there will be the need for a You 3.0 Journey. And let me be the first to tell you, there will be.

How do I know this? Because my personal journey had me go through eight career transitions. And know that each transition required mastery. And that takes years.

Who knows. You may need more transitions, you may need less. Again, your mileage may differ. But more importantly, my journey will continue until it is time to leave this place. Until your time is up, you owe it to yourself to keep learning and growing. For both yourself and for those around you.

As you can tell from reading this book, it is an easy read with incredible amounts of both strategic and tactical support. So a final recommendation I have for everyone reading this book would be to re-read it every November before Thanksgiving and follow it up with a "Year In Review" in December, and before Christmas to make sure your implementation tactics are directionally correct for the New Year.

Finally, I want to congratulate you for deciding to implement change in your life. Most people would rather sit on the couch and do nothing. But you took action. You did it! Please know that it has been my absolute pleasure to walk with you on this journey. And I truly hope that we may have the opportunity to meet at some time in the future when I look forward to hearing about your journey.

For now, and until then, happy journeys. And may the winds of mastery and change always be at your back!

Mark Rosche